JENNI RIVERA

The Diva of Banda Music

MICHAEL PUENTE

W9-AXZ-098

This book is available in quantity at special discounts for your group or organization. For further information, contact:

Triumph Books LLC
814 North Franklin Street
Chicago, Illinois 60610
Phone: (312) 337-0747
www.triumphbooks.com

Printed in U.S.A.

ISBN: 978-1-62937-026-2

JENNI RIVERA

THE DIVA OF BANDA MUSIC

CHAPTER ONE:
LA DIVA DE LA BANDA MAKES HISTORY

CHAPTER ONE: LA DIVA DE LA BANDA MAKES HISTORY

SOLD OUT!!

After more than 10 years of performing before crowds from Los Angeles to Mexico City, Jenni Rivera's time had come.

If there was any question of her place as a bona fide international superstar, that was answered in the summer of 2010 in Southern California.

Just miles from her hometown of Long Beach, California, Jenni Rivera, "La Diva de la Banda," took the stage before thousands of screaming fans at L.A.'s Nokia Theatre on August 6, 2010.

Decked out in a shiny black leather jacket with matching baseball cap, Jenni wasted no time giving her fans what they wanted to see: Belting out her best-loved hits on one of the biggest stages.

The Nokia Theatre has hosted some of the most famous entertainers in the world, like Stevie Wonder, Ricky Martin and Katy Perry.

The no-holds-barred Jenni was there to perform hits from her latest album, *La Gran Senora* (The Great Lady).

And she didn't disappoint the sellout audience.

And not for just one night.

But for two!

That feat made Jenni the first female Mexican Banda music artist to sell out the 7,100 seat venue in back-to-back concerts.

When you sell 20 million records, people take notice and want to be close to you.

"Jenni spoke for a segment of the community that doesn't often get heard, single mothers who work hard every

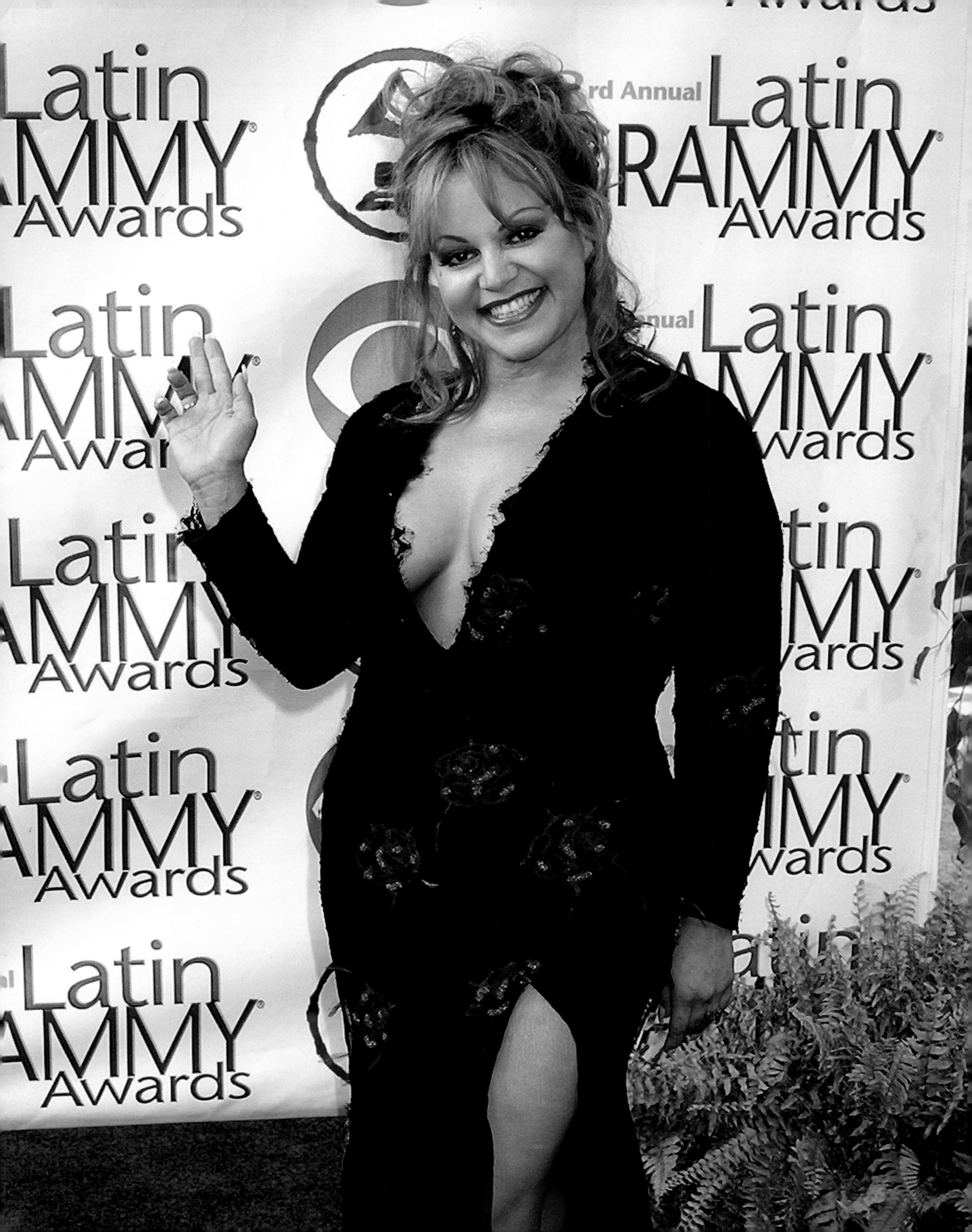
Latin
GRAMMY
Awards

single day, who care for their husbands and families and others but don't get to complain," Flavio Morales, senior vice president of programming and production of NBCUniversal's cable channel, mun2, told the *Los Angeles Times*. "She represented an entire community: Me, my family, my

friends and a whole generation of Mexican Americans who are making up the new America."

In leading up to Jenni's sold out shows at the Nokia Theatre, the Long Beach native continued to impress by shattering records for album sales and award nominations.

In 2009 alone, Jenni earned 7 *Billboard* Award nominations – the most nominations ever for a female regional Mexican music performer.

Whether it be banda, notreña or ranchera music, Jenni dominated and mastered the styles.

With the Nokia Theatre dominated, other renowned venues fell as well: Kodak Theatre, Gibson Amphitheatre, San Jose Convention Center and the Staples Center, home to the Los Angeles Lakers.

For Jenni, she knew her success wasn't by accident, but by hard work and knowing what she wanted.

"I don't want to say I'm a control freak but part of being a control freak is not admitting it," Jenni told the *El Paso Times* in September 2012.

From the lighting to the song selection, Jenni was involved in every aspect of her concerts to give her fans the best and more personal experience.

"I'm involved in everything, whether it's the rundown of my show, when the lights come

on, when there's confetti or fireworks or darkness or videos," Jenni told the *El Paso Times*. "I do it all, which is crazy, I know — but it's my career, my songs, my voice and my audience."

To some, Jenni was seen not just as a Spanish-language performer, but as an inspiration for not giving up when times get tough.

Women found Jenni's example especially inspiring.

"Nowadays, we like and reward a strong female figure in the music industry because it's so hard to make it. People do pay attention to those divas who are able to jump high," said Jorge Vasquez, who helped secure Jenni's concert in El Paso in 2012.

In speaking with the *El Paso Times*, Vasquez added, "A lot of women come to her shows. They feel empowered by Jenni's success. It's an awesome message."

Jenni had her future mapped out and it didn't seem anything could stop her.

"My top goal is to be the Mexican Oprah Winfrey," Jenni said. "I don't want to be a host and be paid for it: I want to own it, like Oprah. I know I have something to say, and people like to listen. I really feel and believe that's what my future will be, but I always thought it would be later on, when I'm done singing and ready to start a new career."

Jenni worked on achieving her goal.

With each new project, her star soared and her popularity continued to climb.

2010 saw the debut of the reality show featuring her daughters, *Jenni Rivera Presents: Chiquis & RaqC.*

Since fans couldn't get enough, 2011 saw the launch of another reality series, *I Love Jenni.*

"My fans love reality. They love for you – for me to be who I am. I'm very transparent. I try to be authentic and genuine with them," Rivera told KTLA.

Following her music and reality shows, cosmetics, fragrances and clothing were the next stop on Jenni's entrepreneurial train.

All of this while Jenni continued to raise her five children: Janney "Chiquis," Jacqui, Michael, Janicka and Johnny.

But while Jenni enjoyed success, she also endured much pain and suffering in her life.

From getting pregnant at the age of 15 with Janney, to being a victim of spousal abuse, to suicide attempts, and other family scandals such as rumors that her third husband, former professional baseball pitcher Esteban Loaiza, had an affair with her daughter, Chiquis.

Through it all, Jenni Rivera endured, persevered and managed to always come out on top.

"I am a woman like any other, and ugly things happen to me like any other woman. The number of times I have fallen down is the number of times I have gotten up," Jenni said at a press conference.

By 2012, Jenni had earned 15 Gold Records, 15 Platinum and 5 Double Platinum Records, with more than 15 million records sold, and a dozen albums released, over a decade, dominating record charts in the United States and Mexico.

According to *Billboard*, TV exposure helped double the average attendance at Jenni's concerts. The magazine reports that in the 2010-11 touring season, attendance at Jenni's concerts rose from "5,085 to 10,262, with average grosses rising nearly 40%, from $329,495 to $460,712. Like regional Mexican acts at the top of their field, Rivera could easily take home $100,000-$200,000 per performance. She toured on weekends, but always tried to be at home early on Sundays when her five children woke up."

Moreover, between 2006 and 2012, fans bought nearly $7 million in tickets, with an overall attendance approaching 120,000. Milestone sellouts at the Nokia Theatre in 2008, 2009 and 2010 led to a landmark

But in the early morning hours of a December day, this bright-shooting comet that was Jenni Rivera, one of the biggest stars in the world, cultural icon, reality TV star, producer, actress, was lost forever.

On December 9, 2012, a plane carrying Jenni and six others fell from the sky and

concert at the Staples Center in 2011 attended by nearly 14,000.

The "Diva de la Banda" had arrived.

"To many people, diva means you're hard to please. To me, a diva is someone that works hard to be at the top of her game," Jenni told *Billboard* in 2011.

crashed in a mountain area near Iturbide, Mexico.

The crash happened shortly after Jenni performed her final sellout concert of her short but brilliant career at Monterrey Arena on December 8 in Monterrey, Nuevo Leon, Mexico.

At 2 a.m. on December 9, following the show, Jenni held a press conference at the same venue.

She and her staff departed for the airport about an hour later. She was scheduled for an appearance in Toluca the next day on the show *La Voz*, the Mexican version of *The Voice*.

By 3:30 a.m., a Learjet took off from the airport near Iturbide, but would soon lose contact with the air traffic control tower.

Soon, Jenni's family, friends and fans worldwide would learn the horrifying news: 43-year-old Dolores Janney "Jenni" Rivera, "La Diva de la Banda," was gone forever.

"I think it's a nightmare. It can't be true," one fan told KCBS-TV in Los Angeles.

Another fan, Claudia Lopez, told the station, "We love her songs. We love her music. We will never forget her."

The unexpected and devastating loss of Jenni Rivera reverberated throughout the world, primarily because of what was expected to come from the still rising star: movies, albums in English and more TV shows.

"For Jenni, it was all about the promise that was yet to come," Morales told the *Los Angeles Times*.

For many, Jenni exuded the message of empowering women.

"Jenni inspired women to believe in themselves and delivered this message in her music," Emily Simonitsch, senior vice president of talent for Live Nation/Southern California, told the *Los Angeles Times*.

From books about her life and other business ventures, the public's appetite for everything and anything Jenni continues after her passing.

"Jenni was heading toward something big and people wanted more," Victor Gonzalez, president of EMLE, the company that distributed Rivera's music under the Fonovisa label, told *Billboard*. Rivera often called Gonzalez for advice. "We realized that no [Latin] celebrity in recent times, not even a politician, has received that kind of coverage. The interest in Jenni illustrates that there was this momentum, a major force. People will continue looking for her in one form or another."

In 2013, The GRAMMY Museum in Los Angeles opened a year-long exhibit on Jenni Rivera's career and life.

It featured Jenni's wardrobe, personal letters and other memorabilia.

"Boasting a discography of over a dozen albums may sound like an easy task to accomplish, but for Jenni Rivera, they represent a labor of love, hard work and most of all, a myriad of sacrifices. And as customary in everything she did, she continued to strive to be simply the best and was always on a quest to give the best of herself to her fans, her family through what she does best, her music," The GRAMMY Museum wrote about Jenni Rivera for its exhibit.

In December 2013, a year after Jenni's untimely death, tributes and concert specials in Mexico helped to keep her memory alive. One concert took place near the crash site in Nuevo Leon, Mexico.

"As a strong Latina, she represented her family, community and state at the

CHAPTER ONE: LA DIVA DE LA BANDA MAKES HISTORY

national and international levels," California State Senator Ricardo Lara (D- Long Beach) said just days after her death. "Her passionate songs of perseverance inspired millions and brought a renewed interest and respect for her interpretations of Mexican

In December 2013, the album *1969 – Siempre, En Vivo Desde Monterrey, Parte 1*, was released as a live album and as a DVD. The album features songs from her last live performance, the night before the plane crashed.

Unfortunately for Jenni and her fans, she joins a list of Mexican-American singers who also died way too young, including Richard Valenzuela, also known as Ritchie Valens, and Tejano music star Selena Quintanilla-Perez. Jenni's untimely death seemed especially tragic, given all that she had overcome. "Although it isn't rare for a prominent celebrity to be honored years – and perhaps decades – after his/her death, Rivera's passing hit harder than most for

regional music to the United States."

Just months after her death, *Unbreakable: My Story, My Way*, Jenni's authorized autobiography, became a *New York Times* bestseller.

And although Rivera is gone, her music lives on.

the Latino community. Her achievements, which include selling millions of albums and being the first female singer of Mexican regional music to sell out various concert venues, speaks volumes when you consider her parents were undocumented immigrants and that she became a mother at 15 years old," reported Biography.com.

"The reality is that Jenni left at the highest moment of her career," Gonzalez said. "She had a strong following and was starting to make new fans who were falling in love with her. She leaves a huge void."

For Jenni, her success was due to all of her hard work, and yet she was still amazed by the support of her fans.

"I'm very happy for the success that I've had, but I guess that I've worked so hard at it; it's not that I feel that I deserve it, but you kind of work hard and you have expectations. So, I'm living my expectations," Jenni told *Billboard*.com in April 2012. "Being a recording artist, selling music, selling concerts out, having a reality show, starting film, it's great, it's beautiful. For people to be watching *I Love Jenni* the way that they are watching it, it's really amazing. It amazes me still that people can be interested in my normal life."

A biopic film on Jenni Rivera by director Francisco Joel Mendoza is filming now and stars Jenni's oldest daughter, Janney "Chiquis" Marin Rivera, as her mother.

SIDEBAR:
LUPILLO RIVERA

SIDEBAR: LUPILLO RIVERA

The first person to receive the call of Jenni Rivera's death was her younger brother and Banda superstar in his own right, Lupillo Rivera. Lupillo was in North Carolina performing when he received the call.

According to Quemas.com, Lupillo was virtually paralyzed when he received the news.

Le llevare su mama a mis sobrinos A nuestra hermana. fans a una gran señora!!!!!!!!!!................ (Mom, I'm going to bring your daughter home; I will bring their mom back to my nieces and nephews, our sister. And fans a great lady!!!!)

Lupillo, who is three years younger than Jenni, was the person who would identify his

Lupillo didn't waste time heading to the home of his mother, Rosa Saavedra, where he quickly took on the role of leader for the family. This is what he tweeted that morning:

"Ama..voy a llevarle a su hija a casa,

sister's remains at a Monterrey hospital.

Announcing to the world the news of his sister's passing wasn't easy.

"We have received 100 percent confirmation that my sister Jenni is gone

to be with the Lord," Lupillo said at a press conference at his mother's home in Lakewood, California, according to *Fox News Latino*. "She is in the presence of God now."

As with many siblings, Lupillo and Jenni had a falling out, but had made up prior to her death.

Quemas.com claims Lupillo reached out to Jenni after her divorce from Major League Baseball player Esteban Loaiza.

The makeup lead to Lupillo and Jenni sharing the stage for the first time in seven years, just 11 days before her death. Jenni declared her undying love for her little brother while performing at the Texcoco, Mexico rodeo on December 1, 2012.

"He's been with me through thick and thin... That's why I'm here today to repay him for everything he's done for me!...Knowing that I have him in my life, and seeing how many of you love him, admire him, applaud him, cry and scream for him, I feel incredibly proud. I feel very fortunate to be his sister," Jenni said.

Months after his sister's death, Lupillo Rivera says his faith helped him get through the ordeal.

Lupillo told *E! News*, "I feel her. I've felt heaviness on my shoulder; I've felt shadows around the stage. It feels good. I like that.

SIDEBAR: LUPILLO RIVERA

... It's never going to be a complete healing. The pain and suffering will always be there. It's my sister, somebody that's not here with us anymore. There will always be an empty spot. Being as we believe in God and we know she's in a better place—that's our satisfaction."

Lupillo was born January 30, 1972 as Guadalupe Rivera in La Barca, Jalisco, Mexico, but grew up in Long Beach, California, like his sister Jenni.

He graduated in 1990 from Long Beach Polytechnic High School. His brother is Pedro Rivera Jr., a Spanish language Christian singer who is also an ordained pastor of Primer Amor.

According to Star Pulse.com, Lupillo actually wanted to be a restaurant owner, not a Banda singer. But his father, Pedro Rivera, the owner of the record label Cintas Acuario, wanted to give his son hands-on experience in the record business. When a contracted singer failed to show up for a recording session, Pedro hired his son to work at the studio.

Lupillo's first job was to go look for talent at local bars, with the notion that some of the acts could be signed to a record contract with his father's label.

According to Univision.com, Lupillo had an encounter in 1990 that would change his life. He met Chalino Sanchez, who gave him

the inspiration and the confidence to sing. He began performing under the nickname "El Toro del Corrido," in honor of his uncle in Mexico, who was a semi-famous professional boxer known as "El Toro Rivera."

At the age of 15, Lupillo wrote his first traditional song dedicated to the memory of Miguel Carlos Ortega, a good friend who passed away. In 1993, he wrote the story "King of the Bars."

Between 1995 and 2012, Lupillo would release 34 albums. His first hit was with a song called "El Moreño."

In 2007, Lupillo was nominated for a Latin Grammy Award for his album *The King of Canteens*. He paid tribute to another legendary Mexican singer, Pedro Infante.

According to Star Pulse.com, Lupillo honored a request from a fallen U.S. Marine who died while in action. The request was for Lupillo to leave one his famous sombreros on the Marine's burial casket during the funeral.

But like his sister, Lupillo is no stranger to controversy. He was accused of leaking intimate photos of him and his wife. Published reports also say Lupillo had ongoing disputes with Jenni's family. to perform to honor his sister's legacy.

"I hope the fans enjoy the shows I'm doing. And I hope they keep on supporting her image, her music, her personality. That's all I ask for," Lupillo told *E! News*.

CHAPTER TWO:
LONG BEACH LIVING

CHAPTER TWO: LONG BEACH LIVING

America has long been seen by immigrants as the destination for a better life. For some, getting here can be a challenge in itself. Despite many obstacles, immigrants risk everything in order to provide their children a better life now and into the future.

That was the goal of Rosa Saavedra and Pedro Rivera when they crossed into the United States from Mexico in the late 1960s.

Pedro Rivera was originally from the Mexican state of Jalisco, while Rosa was from Sonora.

"What's really cool and ironic is my mother was 15 and my father was 16. He left Jalisco, literally on a bicycle. His father wasn't around because he was in the military, so he'd spend two weeks with the family and then he'd be gone for the rest of the year," Jenni told *Open Your Eyes ("OYE") Magazine*. "My father eventually made it to Sonora and started selling lottery tickets at a restaurant in Hermosillo where they were having a 'concurso de aficionados,' a singing contest. My mom was singing. He fell in love with her and her voice."

Once the couple arrived at Long Beach, they found out that Rosa was expecting her first child.

That child, Dolores Janney Rivera, was born on July 2, 1969 in Long Beach, California. She would later become known as Jenni.

"I wasn't born with a silver spoon in my mouth. My parents were immigrants. They were pregnant with me when they crossed the border illegally. I was the first one born in the United States. They came to this country to give my brothers a better life and here they were pregnant with me," Jenni told *Billboard* in 2011. "My mom was very honest when she told me, 'Mija, I tried all kinds of home remedies for you not to be born, but you were a survivor since then.'"

For Jenni and her family, noticeable

where Pedro and Rosa raised Jenni and her four brothers and sister in a tight-knit household. Her brother Lupillo is also an award winning regional Mexican musician.

In the family's bilingual household, Pedro introduced Jenni to their traditional Mexican music: Banda, a brass, polka style popularized in Northern Mexico and with Mexican immigrants in the United States. They also enjoyed the Norteña and Ranchera styles of Mexican music.

"Mexican music runs through my veins. I love it. Growing up, my father didn't allow us to listen to English music at home. That's all I heard. I had no choice. As I got older, Banda started coming in and I started liking it," Jenni said.

It was also during this time when her father worked as a bartender and business man. According to the *London Times*, Pedro Rivera worked in factories by day and sang corridos in the nightclubs in and around Los Angeles at night. He discovered that he had a gift for writing topical corridos (ballads), about issues such as the Gulf War of the 1990s to the Los Angeles riots following the acquittal

success would still be years away after their arrival to the United States.

It was on the West Side of Long Beach

of the police officers who were accused of beating motorist Rodney King in 1992.

While her father was working and singing, Jenni was in high school. In 1984, during her sophomore year at Long Beach Polytechnic High School, Jenni, a straight A student, got pregnant by her boyfriend, Trino Marin. Janney Marin Rivera would be Jenni's first of five children.

As a result, her parents kicked her out of the house. In an interview with the *Los Angeles Times*, Jenni spoke about never giving up.

"Usually, when a young girl is pregnant, she drops out of school and concentrates on being a mother. I thought that's what I had to do, but my counselors told me there was no way they would let me drop out," Jenni said. "I had too much promise."

She eventually married Trino and the couple had two more children, Jacqueline, born in 1989, and Michael, born in 1991. However, more children didn't lead to more happiness. In their eight years of marriage, Trino was difficult and challenging.

According to published reports, Jenni says Trino was physically and mentally abusive toward her. Problems in her marriage led to depression, giving Jenni a sense of hopelessness. She tried taking her life on at least two occasions.

Jenni somehow found the strength to leave her husband and made peace with her parents. The bottom dropped out in 1992 when Jenni discovered that Marin had molested their daughters, Chiquis and Jacqui, along with Jenni's younger sister, Rosie. The marriage between Jenni and

Marin ended in 1992 after the molestation accusations.

Criminal charges were filed in 1997 and Marin was listed as a fugitive for nine years before being apprehended in April 2006. He was eventually convicted of sexual assault and rape and sentenced to more than 30 years in prison.

Even during this tough time, Jenni managed to earn her GED and graduated as the valedictorian of a continuation school in Long Beach. Following high school, Jenni attended Long Beach City College and California State University in Long Beach where she studied business administration. To support herself and her child, Jenni sold CDs at flea markets while her father sold cassettes at car washes.

"We had our own music stands in the local swap meets. We sold cassette tapes at the time, and that's how we made a living," Rivera told *Billboard*. "We stepped it up a bit when my father opened his own record store and eventually started his own record label."

"I went to school to study business administration. I never imagined I would be marketing myself," Jenni said. Upon graduating from college, Jenni started selling

real estate in the Long Beach area.

Before long, she started helping out at her father's recording studio and record label that he started called Cintas Acuario.

"I never wanted to become a singer. My dad would take me to singing lessons when I was little, but I loved school. I got good grades because I thought education was important," Jenni told oyemag.com. "Time passed and I graduated from high school. Then I went to college and majored in business management. I became a real estate agent, and pretty successful, working part-time. Then the label grew and my dad asked my brother and me if we would come and help out, so I would basically do everything, from answering the phones to handling sales and legal issues."

Pedro Rivera pushed his five children to get involved in every aspect of the recording business, the *London Times* reported. As his label grew more successful, he encouraged his son Lupillo and Jenni into the spotlight, since they both grew up speaking English and listening to pop music. With the insistence of their father, Lupillo and Jenni recorded traditional Mexican music, believing this was the kind of music that Los Angeles' huge Mexican population wanted to hear.

She discovered a new dream, but not right away. Jenni Rivera launched her musical dynasty on a dare. "The first time I got on stage was in 1993, a few months after the father of my first three children and I had separated. ... When we split up, my friends picked me up and took me to a nightclub called El Rancho Grande in Carson, California. That's the night I discovered tequila. A single mother who had never gone out before, in a nightclub with tequila, wasn't a good mix," Rivera told *Billboard*.

"My friends dared me to go onstage and sing. I was a little tipsy and sang 'Las Nieves de Enero' by Chalino Sanchez, who had passed away close to a year before. After I was done, all the other drunken people applauded me. I liked it. Since my dad wanted me to be an artist, I figured he already had a recording label. Maybe I could

have access to the musicians and the studio. That's when I started recording."

Jenni described her first recording to *OYE*. "My father had been asking me to record for a while, so I did just that. I prepared a whole album and turned it into him on DAT (Digital Audio Tape)."

"Here Dad, Happy Birthday! Here's what you've always wanted!" Jenni said.

Giving her father the DAT he'd been longing for turned into a big deal. Soon they began to turn out a new CD every year, and it wasn't too long before Jenni's powerful voice and songs were getting airplay all over L.A.

"Well, every year, he (Jenni's dad) wanted another album and there I was. He planted a picture on it and [it] sold 15 units a year.

In 1999, one of those CDs, *Reina de las Reinas*, started getting airplay on K-Buena. On La Ley, which is now La Raza, 97.9, they started playing 'Las Maladrinas'," Jenni said. "While I was driving my clients to see a house — they started playing my music! And the next half hour, people were like, 'Can we hear that song again from that one girl?' The CD started selling, then the nightclub owners and promoters started calling to ask if I would perform. When they talked about paying me for this, I said, 'Hey, I can do this for a little while and I can come back to real estate later.' From 1999 on, that's when I took my career seriously."

"I had no choice but to work hard. ... I never thought I was going to be a singer myself. It came accidentally," Jenni told *Billboard*. "When I started getting called for events at local nightclubs, I'd leave the kids with the

babysitter and go to work and make $100. All I wanted to do was bring cheese, tortillas, beans and whatever else I could get for the refrigerator."

A star would eventually be born, but there was much work to be done if she wanted to hit it big in banda music, a music genre often reserved for macho men. Banda music is a traditional form of

CHAPTER TWO: LONG BEACH LIVING

Mexican music that is popular in cities with large Mexican-American populations such as Los Angeles, Houston, Dallas and Chicago. It's also very male dominated, as the Mexican culture historically tends to be. Singing a style of music that was usually reserved for men wasn't easy.

"At first, it was pretty difficult. I didn't get a lot of respect because I was the only female artist to stand out. They wouldn't program my music," Jenni told *OYE*. "I would go to the program directors at the radio stations and say, 'I'm my own priority.' I think they just got tired of me coming by so they would eventually program my material."

Jenni performed in both Spanish and English, addressing personal themes such as her struggles with violence, weight issues and divorce. Initially, Jenni sang ballads, but in the mid-1990s, she joined Lupillo in singing narcocorridos, a sort of underground form of Banda music that some say glorified L.A.'s gang and drug underworld, similar to gangsta rap.

"More established Latin record labels were ignoring this underground music form. Indeed, Cintas Acuario had made its initial fortune with recordings of Chalino, a narcocorrido singer whose brief, brutal life would make him an icon to young Mexican-Americans," the *London Times* reported in late 2012. Soon, Lupillo and Jenni were the most sought after young Mexican singers in Los Angeles, and their fame would soon spread to Chicago, Dallas and Phoenix, cities with large Mexican immigrant populations.

In 1994, Jenni wrote her first corrido called "La Chacalosa." "I was telling a story about a female drug dealer who learned the business from her father," Jenni told *Billboard*. "At the time, corridos were hardcore. I figured if I'm the only female who's going to sing one, it's going to attract attention. People still love it to this day." She released her first album, *Chacalosa* (Spanish slang for "party girl"), under the Brentwood record label in 1995.

On the cover, she was sporting a cowboy hat and showing off her sexy cleavage while standing in front of a low-ride pickup truck. The songs from Chacalosa like "Woman Can," "Open Book," and "Smuggler Bitch," told corrido stories.

In an interview with writer Elijah Ward in 1999, Jenni spoke about why she penned corridos. "I wrote my first corrido in '94 because I knew it would catch attention.

All the men were doing it and girls are bad girls too, you know. Not only do they like to listen to the music, but there are women drug dealers. So, I figured we were being left aside," she said.

When asked by Wood if she thought her music was glorifying gangs and criminals, Jenni replied, "We've always defended our point of view by the fact that we've never used drugs, we've never sold drugs. We grew up around this. We didn't grow up in rich neighborhoods. We grew up in the ghetto."

Jenni's inspiration for writing her music was her fans.

"My inspiration is always what I think my fans want to listen to. I often write about social problems. If I'm not going through it or I haven't gone through it, I want to make sure it touches someone," Jenni told *Billboard*. "That's what I base my music on. I'm really in touch with my fans. Through their emails, letters and stories is how I decide what music I'm going to perform."

That's how she approached her single, "Las Malandrinas," she said. "It was the late 1990s and the early 2000s and the female singers were singing ballads and romantic fare. So I figured, I'm not typical at all in any way, so

sentenced to six months in prison for smuggling immigrants. Despite the downturn in her marriage, Jenni's music began to soar. Spanish radio stations throughout Southern California began giving Jenni's music significant airplay.

In the late 1990s, Jenni signed with Sony Records and then with Fonovisa Records in 1999. She released her first commercial album with Fonovisa, titled *Que Me Entierren con la Banda*, featuring the hit "Las Malandrinas." In 2001, Jenni released the singles "Dejate Amar" and "Se las Voy a Dar a Otro." Fonovisa also released Homenajea a Las Grandes, which means homage to the great ones. It was Rivera paying tribute to famous Mexican female singers such as Lucho Villa, Mercedes Castro, Rocio Durcal, Lola Beltran and Alejandra Guzman.

From here, Jenni moved ever so closer to her final destination of being "La Diva de la Banda."

I'm going to do what the guys do but in a different voice."

She eventually signed to Capitol/EMI's Latin division in 1994, which led to other recordings. She also independently released the albums *We Are Rivera* and *Farewell to Selena*, which is sadly ironic since Selena, a performer of Tejano music, died early into her music career when she was shot by an obsessed fan in 1995.

Jenni was performing in bars when she met Juan Lopez. The two were married in 1997, but shortly after that Lopez was

SIDEBAR:

STARS REACT
TO LOSS OF JENNI

SIDEBAR: STARS REACT TO LOSS OF JENNI

The loss of Jenni Rivera on that fateful December 2012 day was felt by her fans all over the world, including by some of the biggest names in music, film and sports, both in the United States, Mexico and beyond.

Many celebrities quickly took to Twitter when Jenni's tragic death was confirmed.

Here are just some of the examples:

"What terrible news! Rest in peace...My deepest condolences for her family and friends," wrote Mexican singer and actress Lucero.

Mexican pop star Paulina Rubio, who sat alongside Rivera on the *La Voz*, the Mexican version of the show *The Voice* wrote: "My friend! Why? There is no consolation. God, please help me!"

Mexican-American actress Eva Longoria was shocked to learn about the death Jenni: "My heart breaks for the loss of Jenni Rivera & everyone on the plane. My prayers go out to her family. We lost a legend today."

TV star Mario Lopez, host of the singing competition *The X Factor*, was saddened by the news. "Spent some time with Jenni Rivera recently. What an amazing lady... Cool, smart, funny & talented. Such a travesty... God Bless her family," he wrote.

Meanwhile, Jennifer Lopez wrote on Twitter, "So sad! Praying for Jenni Rivera's children and family and the passengers' families."

Pitbull, a close friend and collaborater of Lopez, added his own thoughts: "I highly respected #JenniRivera 4 being a gr8 performer but more than that being real & gr8 example 4 us all que dios la bendiga & may she RIP."

Legendary singer and songwriter Gloria Estefan, who herself had a brush with death earlier in her career, reacted this way: "OMG! Just heard about @jennirivera praying for her and her family during this difficult & uncertain time! Our deepest sympathy to the family & fans of @jennirivera & those who accompanied her on what was to be her last voyage. Rest in peace..."

Mexican singer Thalia: "Oh my God! I just found out about the terrible news of Jenni Rivera. I'm praying for a miracle! A chain of prayers for Jenni and her family.

Mexican singer Gloria Trevi: "Keep praying for Jenni and her companions, please! Strength and love for their families."

"Heard confirmed news about our dear @JenniRivera.. this breaks my heart in a million pieces.. it is just a huge loss for our community," said Mexican-American actor Wilmer Valderrama. "Your story, ur passion, ur pride 4 ur family & ur latino community

inspired us all. U leave behind the legacy of an icon #RIPJenniRivera," he added.

Because Jenni's fame had reached into mainstream America, many non-Latino celebrities expressed sadness upon learning of her sudden passing.

"RIP #JenniRivera blessed I got to know u the past few years. Talented, humble, smart, cool as f**k. My kind of diva," *Late Call* TV host Carson Daly wrote on his Twitter account.

Def Jam, hip hop music label co-founder Russell Simmons wrote, "RIP Jenni Rivera."

LaToya Jackson, sister of the late Michael Jackson, wrote: "#Jenni was such an inspiration to so many & definitely made an impact in the Hispanic community! RIP Jenni Rivera!"

SIDEBAR: STARS REACT TO LOSS OF JENNI

TV star Kirstie Alley: "RIP Jenni Rivera...and God bless your children."

Even the Los Angeles Dodgers baseball team, where Jenni had performed the National Anthem at a game, wrote "Rest in Peace, Jenni Rivera."

Legondary American crooner Tony Bennett, who performed in Mexico City the night after Jenni's passing, wrote: "My performance tonight in Mexico City is dedicated to the wonderful artist Jenni Rivera and everybody involved in yesterday's tragedy."

American pop princess Christina Aguilera, and co-host of *The Voice*, wrote "#TheVoice & Latin community has lost someone so talented & special. Thoughts & prayers are with you all as we mourn the loss of Jenni Rivera."

American Idol host Ryan Seacrest: "@ jessimaldonado thank u for sharing your stories of @jennirivera... amazing how she inspired so many."

American rapper Snoop Dogg: "Rip jenni rivera- sweet lady n a beautiful voice she will b missed we were supposed to do a song together Im so sad!"

American TV host Ellen DeGeneres: "I know a lot of my followers have been saddened by the news about Jenni Rivera. Sending love to her family and her fans."

American actor John Leguizamo: "#jenni rivera is a tragedy. Please artists dont fly those lil planes. They always get us."

Oscar winning actress and co-host of *The View*, Whoopi Goldberg wrote: "R.I.P. Jenni Rivera, AMAZING & very talented woman.

My deep condolence to her family... Love her music."

Mexican singer Mijares: "Abrazos, oraciones y mi mas sentido pesame para todos los deudos de @jennirivera y acompañantes en este terrible accidente." (Hugs, prayers and my deepest condolences for all the relatives of @Jennirivera and companions in this terrible accident)

Kat DeLuna: "Let's pray for @jennirivera and for the ones who were on her plane. God please give her family strength during this moment."

Joan Sebastian: "AMIGA! Aplaudire llorando por la conclucion de tu vida terrenal y por el inicio de tu INMORTALIDAD!" (FRIEND! I will applaud as I cry for the conclusion of your earthly life and for the beginning of your IMMORTALITY!)

Vikki Carr: "Pls everyone say a prayer for Jenni Rivera. Died in airplane crash with her group in Mexico. God grant her peace. So shocked and sad."

Pepe Aguilar: "Sinceramente no tengo palabras. Completa y sincera solidaridad para todos los familiares de las victimas de esta tragedia...... ...muy especialmente......para todos sus fans. Descanse en paz. Importante reflexionar sobre lo fragiles que somos. La vida es una bendicion, nuestro mayor y unico tesoro.....jamas hay que olvidarlo." (Sincerely I don't have words. Complete and sincere solidarity for the families of the victims of this tragedy, most especially, for all their fans. Rest in peace. Important to reflect on how fragile we are. Life is a blessing, our greatest and sole treasure ... we must never forget it.)

Mariana Ochoa from the pop group OV7: "Me uno a las oraciones.. Q noticia tan terrible. Sin palabras..." (I join the prayers. What terrible news. There are no words...)

Edith Marquez: "Sigo impactada por esta triste noticia !!! Bendiciones para sus hijos !!!! Jenni Rivera te vamos a extranar!!!! Y mucho." (I'm still shocked by this sad news! Blessings for your children!! Jenni Rivera will miss you!!)

CONQUERING A MAN'S WORLD

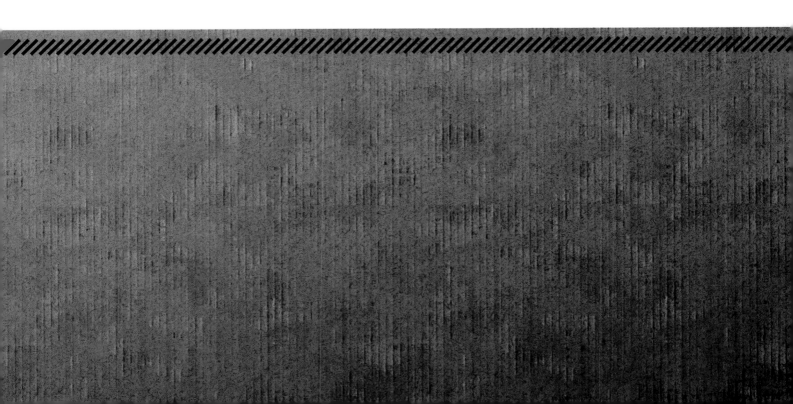

In Mexican culture, women are expected to behave much differently than men. They're not supposed to swear, drink or flirt. And, if they do any of those things, they're not supposed to talk about it, much less sing about it.

But if a man can do it, than why not a woman?

Jenni Rivera would be that woman.

"I found it improper a mujer would sing about getting drunk and flirting around and being proud of it, especially in a genre and culture in which females were expected to be classy damas," wrote Gustavo Arellano, a respected writer of Mexican music and culture.

Arellano interviewed Rivera for three hours in 2003, the first time the Mexican music critic had ever spoken to her.

He was skeptical about her. Especially since, at that time, he had not heard much about her.

"Over the course of that conversation, I dropped all my macho bullshit and became an eternal fan. It wasn't just the music, which was loud, brash and wonderfully unapologetic, but also what she represented: a visionary who, as I would write, 'changed Mexican culture forever' simply by singing about her rags-to-riches story and urging fans to believe they also could find success if they only tried," Arellano wrote.

As Arellano saw it, Rivera had an opportunity to do what no other artist was doing in the Mexican music industry:

CHAPTER THREE: CONQUERING A MAN'S WORLD

"Telling the stories of Mexicans outside the traditional Madonna/whore prism."

"I became a singer because I'm a businesswoman," Rivera told Arellano. "I was a business child, then a business teenager, and finally a businesswoman. No other woman was doing it, so I knew I'd dominate the market."

changing. Mexican women no longer just sit there, expecting men to support us. We can't anymore—it's too expensive. Either you get off your ass and make something of yourself or you starve."

According to Arellano, Jenni got things started with what he described as "novelty singles" — "La Chacalosa" and "Las

"At the same time, I didn't just want to be another pretty body onstage," Rivera continued in the OC Weekly. "I wanted to convey a message—that women could be as bad-ass as men. Look, Mexican society is going to be macho forever because that's just how our culture is. But with so many people moving to the United States, it's

Malandrinas." The songs translate to "The Jackal Woman" and "The Bad Girls." The songs sought to "scandalize Mexican society in the late 1990s," Arellano wrote.

Then came her hit "Ovarios," an attempt to force society to look at ovaries the same way it uses the expression "balls" to signify strength or bravery.

wanted to be; the American success story Mexican immigrants want for their children," Arellano continued.

Jenni attributed much of her early success in music to narcocorridos — a genre that her fans identified with, but is controversial.

"I'm just like them. I think they're tired of seeing these fabricated artists who, yeah, they're fine, they're beautiful, but how many of our fans look like that, you know what I'm saying? Not only in the looks, but they can identify with me because I came from the 'hood, I came from the ghetto – that's who buys my music. It's the humble people," Jenni said just a few years after she made her debut.

Arellano writes, "Her's (Jenni) was a tough life—three divorces, a domestic-violence survivor, weatherer of continued snips by doubters who saw her as simultaneously too hood and too low-class Mexican—but it was hers, and she performed it without shame."

"And that's what endeared her so much," Arellano wrote, "to millions of Mexican women and more than a few males."

"Rivera was the cousin whom the tías always clucked about; the prima who was a bit too loud, a bit too independent, but successful; the type of woman everyone

Marty Preciado, a writer with *Remezcla*, wrote in December 2013 that Jenni Rivera's music and style crafted a new image of the Mexican female. She used the male-dominated genre of Banda music for her own needs and to get her own message across.

"Jenni Rivera had the courage to challenge the idealized notions of beauty promoted

CHAPTER THREE: CONQUERING A MAN'S WORLD

in Anglo culture, where thin and fair skin occupies a privileged space in the music industry," Preciado wrote. "She became pivotal in cementing new parameters of

frequently objectified and undermined as potential artists in the genre. She was one of the few females to sing narcocorridos," Preciado wrote.

Jenni believes the real Jenni Rivera, the one who would go on to become "La Diva de la Banda," was born when Fonovisa released the song "Las Malandrinas." It was a single from her album, *Que Me Entierren Con la Banda* in 1999.

"'Las Malandrinas' is a musical gem and anthem that began to tear the ideological status quo regarding how women's behavior was viewed," Preciado wrote. "A song which perfectly depicts the desire of a woman to be an

identity and female empowerment by defining new values for a chingona (hot shot woman) and being a source of inspiration for women, who, like her, were undergoing considerable personal strife."

"In the narcocorrido musical sphere, women were placed in dark corners,

agent of her desires and enjoy life, without having to cater to misogynist views."

"Rivera's female empowerment discourse is a demonstration of her profound influence across and beyond music. She embraced her barrio upbringing and deeply rooted cultural traditions by integrating her values

into her music. She continues to serve as a cultural text and inspiration to the marginalized women who face machismo in their day-to-day lives," wrote Preciado. Jenni Rivera is a "woman who roared in a male-dominated genre, paving the way for the empowerment and liberation of barrio women."

According to Jenni, 'Las Maladrinas' was when "Jenni Rivera the artist was actually born."

This is what Jenni herself had to say about the song. "'Malandrinas' means 'bad girls,' but not bad in a negative way. I wrote it in homage to my female fans. The type of girls who go clubbing, drink tequila and stand up for themselves."

Rivera credits Fonovisa/Universal with successfully marketing "Las Malandrinas." Rivera had just switched to Fonovisa/Universal from Sony, a big move in her career.

"At the time, Sony was very successful and had a long list of artists who were more successful than me, regional Mexican musicians like my brother (Lupillo Rivera) and other artists who my father had licensed out to them," Rivera told *Billboard*. "I needed to get out of there and go somewhere that I could get more attention."

Still, obtaining the respect and admiration of her male counterparts wasn't easy.

Sometimes even her own father, Pedro Rivera, founder of the record label Cintas Acuario, and Lupillo Rivera, Jenni's Grammy Award-winning brother who is a narcocorrido icon in his own right, had difficulty convincing those who didn't believe she could do it.

"She did just that by refusing to play the stereotypical submissive female, instead casting herself as an outspoken, tequila-imbibing feminist," *Billboard* reported. "The key to Rivera's longevity has always been her authenticity, from the moment she first grabbed a microphone as a divorced mother of three trying to pay the bills to her present-day status as a multi-hyphenated performer who is really a businesswoman at heart."

Jenni said that the naysayers actually pushed her to begin singing seriously, after

only doing it on the side for years.

"I've been recording since 1993. It was a hobby for six of those years. In 1999, I decided to do it full time and take it seriously. When I started getting so many haters and closed doors, I decided to prove that it could be done. I was a divorced single mother of three at the time and a size 12-not your typical model artist who labels feel work for the music industry," Jenni told *Billboard* in 2011. "There were so many no's because of my music, how I looked and because I decided to enter a male-dominated genre. They thought that I was crazy. The adversity and struggles ended up being my blessing. That is where my following came from. My fans would say, 'She's really like us. She looks like us. She talks like us. She acts like us. She goes through what we go through.' Here I am 13 years later.'"

Just getting airplay back then was a struggle for Jenni.

"It's a male-dominated genre. It was hard knocking on those doors to get my music played. One radio programmer in L.A., the meanest son of a bitch in the world, threw my CD in the trash right in my face. I'm glad I went through that because it gave me the gas to keep going," Jenni said. "It made me say, 'One day, I'll prove to this guy that I can make it.'"

Even as Jenni was breaking down barriers and smashing stereotypes, she didn't shy away from showing a softer side in her music. She did so in the song, "Amiga Si Lo Ves." However, it didn't mean Jenni was starting to move away from her bread and butter, the rougher corridos.

"I don't think I can move away from that because if I do, who else is going to do it? If I leave, my crowd would kill me. They want somebody to represent them and that's me," Jenni told bantanga.com. "So, if I can stay with them and give them what they want, yet still be able to conquer a new market, then that's the ideal thing for me."

Jenni said she did not see herself as a role model for other young women.

"I think I've had to be (a role model). I didn't want to consider myself that, but that's what I've become. I've gotten to where I am because I'm different, because I'm daring, because I represent my people. I love them," Jenni told Bantanga.com. "And because I'm real, they figure, 'Wow! Jenni has been through this, just like I was, and Jenni has done this, just like I did.' I've been through all kinds of things, just like my fans have. I became a role model and now I love it. It makes me more aware, makes me more careful as to what I'm going to do."

The key to Rivera's success in this genre of music wasn't her powerful and sultry voice, says Los Angeles music journalist and author Agustin Gurza. It was her storytelling that came through her personal experience, he said.

"It was that she poured her life story into her songs, with all her faults, downfalls and tragedies, including teen pregnancy and domestic abuse," Gurza told the *Miami Herald*. "The fans made her a star because they saw themselves reflected in her."

Singing about drinking, having fun and doing what most proper women wouldn't dare connected her with fans on both sides of the border.

"She was the first Mexican-American female singer from Southern California to achieve superstardom on both sides of the border, and that success inspired the legion of fans who shared her immigrant roots and humble working-class upbringing," Gurza said. "What set Jenni apart was

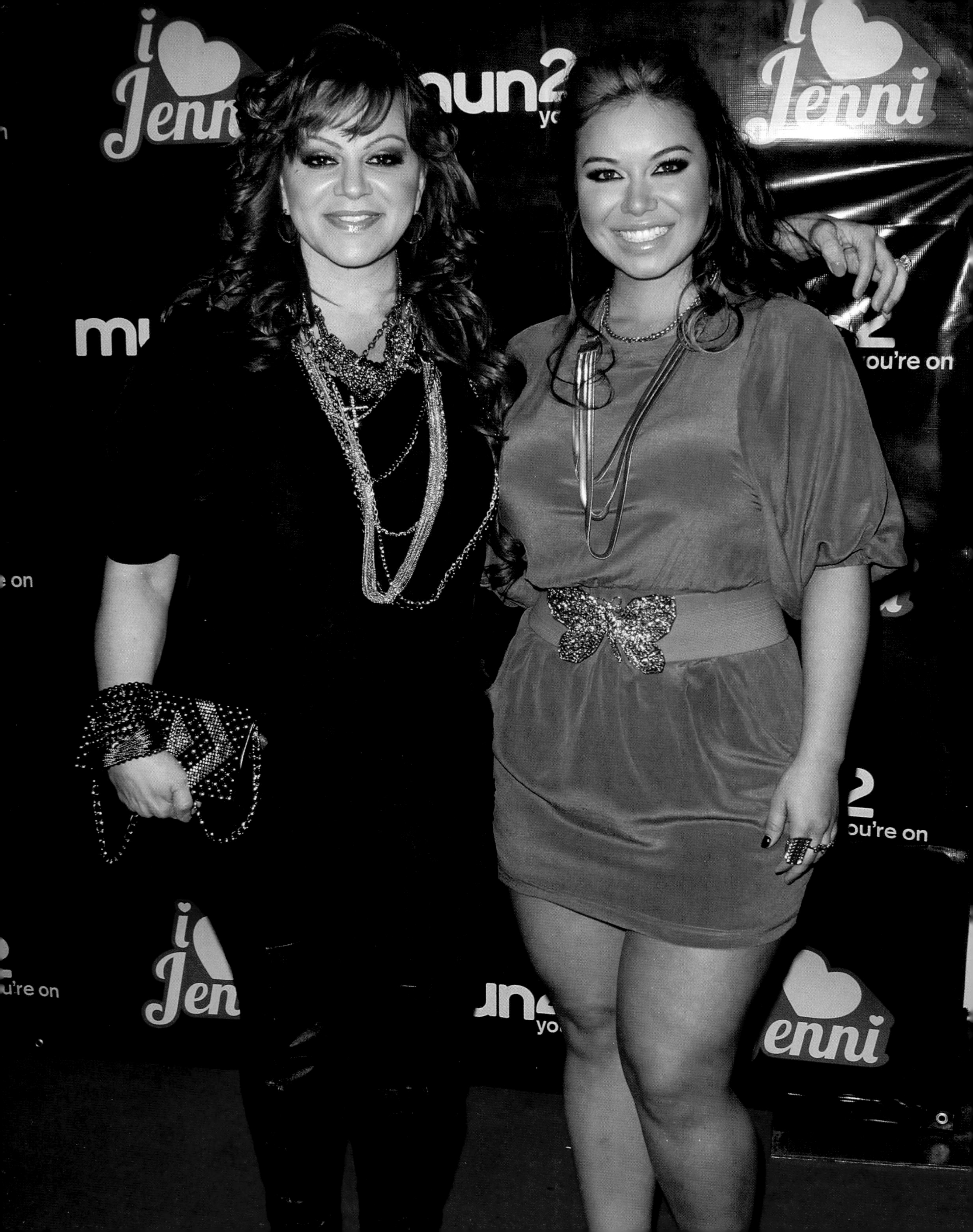

i Jenni
you're on

her willingness to expose her personal life, including those sometimes sordid episodes. Hers was a story of working-class triumph, of poor people beating the odds, of perseverance and guts in the face of adversity. Fans can't get enough of that, because it gives them hope for their own

ability to overcome all their hardships and stumbling blocks."

For some, it's amazing the level of success Jenni achieved "while being caught in a sort of no-man's land: For many, she was not American enough for American audiences or Mexican enough for Mexican audiences," said Gabriel Abaroa Jr., president and CEO of the Latin Recording Academy. "And yet, by the force of her talent and personality

she did it — and she was massive. She'd just as soon fill an auditorium or a concert hall as she would fill a soccer stadium or a bull ring."

While many say Jenni broke down barriers for women in Mexican music, but that's where Gurza disagrees with them. Gurza is the author of *The Strachwitz Frontera Collection of Mexican and Mexican American Recordings.*

"She (Jenni) fits within a long and respected tradition of successful female singers dating back to the Revolution, including Lucha Reyes in the 1930s and more recently Lola Beltran, Amalia Mendoza, Yolanda del Rio and the late Chavela Vargas," Gurza told the *Miami Herald.*

The OC *Weekly*'s Arellano says Jenni knew where she wanted to go and how to get there.

"They're going to think of a woman who's real. They'll think about a woman who went through hell and back and never gave up. No one else has ever opened doors for me—I opened them myself," Jenni told Arellano. "And people have a problem with women who do that. They have a problem when we're no longer as passive and submissive as, say, their mothers were growing up. Too bad. I say what I say, and I do what I do. I'm me."

WHAT IS BANDA, NORTEÑA AND RANCHERA?

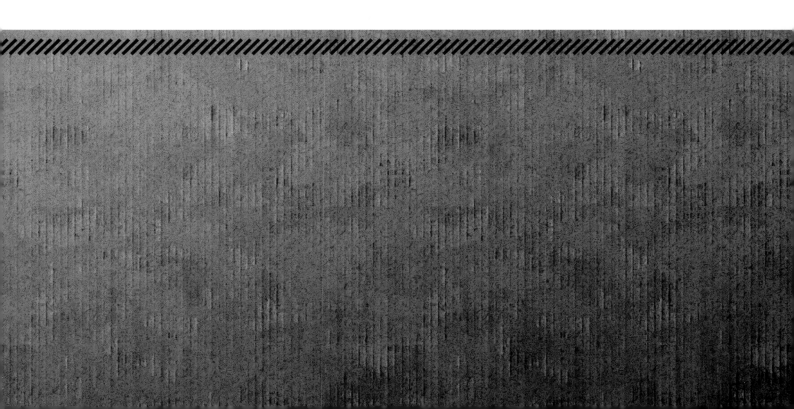

SIDEBAR: WHAT IS BANDA, NORTEÑA AND RANCHERA?

Exactly what are Banda, Norteña and Ranchera musical styles?

Aren't these Mexican musical styles that the "Diva de la Banda" Jenni Rivera sang pretty much all the same?

The short answer: No!

are also different from each other.

So, here's a little Mexican musical history lesson for you.

Let's start with Banda...

"At various times in Mexico, one can hear the sound of Mexican Banda playing from blocks away. Its militant brass rips through the air like shrapnel and the driving bass drum and cymbal seem to loosen the foundations of buildings. As one approaches closer, through the rising dust and fury, one can feel the ground shake with determined vibrancy," writes Don Bergland, Associate of Arts Education at the University of Victoria in Canada.

Asking that question is akin to wondering if rap music is the same as big band music or if jazz is the same as the blues.

Just as there are many forms of American music, the same is true in Latin Music.

At the outset, let's understand what Banda or Norteña and Ranchera is not.

It isn't salsa, merengue, bachata, Tejano, bolero, or bassa nova, which are some of the popular Latin musical styles heard all over the United States, Mexico and Latin America.

To be fair, Banda, Norteña and Ranchera

"The bass drummer pummels his equipment with possessive fury. Trombones and trumpets stand upright, projecting a brass intensity as cutting as any phalanx of war spears, while the armored roar of a tuba rolls beneath a fusillade of staccato peck horns. All this is performed with a passionate enthusiasm that leaves most non-Mexicans either shaking their heads in terror or beating a hasty retreat towards solitude."

A Banda band ranges in size from around 8 to 24 members, consisting of mainly brass or wind instruments like clarinets, trumpets, trombones and tubas and, sometimes, a lot of drums.

"Most often a Banda-like band with an accordion is actually a Norteña band. While some Norteña does come from Sinaloa, most comes from the more northern states of Mexico. Norteña can also thank the Germans (and the Czechs) for its beginnings. It is more of a rural sound," Saphiere says.

When it comes to the Banda "sound," there are several different types, the most common being cumbias, rancheras and corridos.

The most famous and best example is Banda El Recodo, Saphiere says. "The full name of the band is Banda Sinaloense el Recodo de Don Cruz Lizárraga. The band has been under the control and guidance of the Lizárraga family for over 70 years. Their current lead singer sounds very different than the last singer, but he is great and is very young and hopefully will be the primary voice of Banda El Recodo for years to come."

Other popular Banda bands include La Arrolladora Banda El Limon, Banda MS, Cuisillos, Banda Jerez and Banda Los

Bergland writes that Banda music isn't for everyone.

"Although Mexicans themselves gather and applaud these Banda performances with passion, non-Mexican folks seem to avoid them with equal passion," Bergland writes. "The music is very loud and brassy and the driving percussion is sometimes quite demanding. The ferocity of brass playing and the dissonance of intonation and tuning is sometimes quite unnerving to unsuspecting ears. As a result, Mexican Banda music seems to be an uncomfortably acquired taste for people foreign to the culture."

According to Mexico-based writer Dianne Hofner Saphiere, Banda is popular in Mazatlan and the rest of Sinaloa, the state where the music originated.

"Banda style music dates back to the late 1800s. It was imported from Germany when the Germans came over to invent Pacifico beer," Saphiere said.

SIDEBAR: WHAT IS BANDA, NORTEÑA AND RANCHERA?

"Although the people of Mexico listen to music from all over the world and also produce their own forms of modern music, traditional Mexican music continues to be very popular with people of all ages. These traditional forms of Mexican music are undeniably colorful, filled with passion and were created in the origins of this culturally rich country."

Some popular Norteña artists include Los Alegres de Teran, Los Cachorros De Juan Villarreal, Los Tigres del Norte, and Los Tucanes de Tijuana.

Now, concerning Ranchera music...

It literally means "Ranch music," and is a simpler form of Mexican music. Like Banda, its beginnings date back to the Mexican Revolution.

Basically, Ranchera uses an acoustic guitar and some occasional horns. Like many forms of music, Ranchera lyrics center on love and lost love.

Many Ranchera singers wear cowboy attire when performing to look like the Mexican horsemen who inspired the music, complete with a jacket, gun, holsters, tight boots and a large sombrero.

According to Gustavo Arellano of the OC *Weekly*, some of the greatest Ranchera singers of all time include Vicente Fernandez, Pedro Infante, Lola Beltran, Jorge Negrete, Antonio Aguilar, and Javier Solis.

Recoditos, all of which are male groups.

Popular female Banda singers include Victoria Ortiz, Carmen Jara, Ana Bárbara, Graciela Beltrán, Korina Lopez and of course, "La Diva de la Banda," Jenni Rivera.

Next, onto Norteña music...

It's a bit different than Banda, and its origins begin in Northern Mexico (Norteño means Northern) and southern Texas along the border of the United States and Mexico.

The main ingredient for Norteña is the use of one or more accordions.

"In the late 19th century European migrants brought the accordion, waltz and polka, from their homeland to Northern Mexico and the U.S. Southwest. Local bands adopted these elements, blended them with their Ranchera music, and a new genre was born. The tempo is usually middle or fast. 'Tejano' or 'Tex-Mex' music is often confused with Norteña, however Tejano is a blend of Norteña and American rock and country according to haciendatresrios.com.

MUSICIAN BY NIGHT, BUSINESSWOMAN BY DAY

Jenni Rivera, "La Diva de la Banda," was the Queen of Regional Mexican music, more specifically the genres of Banda, Norteña and Ranchera. She dominated the music charts in the United States and Mexico for more than a decade.

"I'm a woman of goals and accomplishments. I've accomplished a whole lot in my music career. Now my heart is set on having a TV and radio show. I want to be able to talk to the people that love me and get paid for it," Jenni Rivera told *Billboard Magazine* in 2011. "I want to be the

There was simply no one like her and replacing her won't be easy.

But even if her music style can be copied, mimicked and replicated, duplicating Jenni's business sense and savvy is unlikely.

You see, Jenni wasn't just a musical force, but a business one as well.

Mexican-American Oprah Winfrey. That's what my goal has always been." From fragrances, to jeans, sportswear, cosmetics and hair products, Jenni wasn't only a musician, she had become a brand.

"I am more of a businesswoman. That's what I've always been. Since I

CHAPTER FOUR: MUSICIAN BY NIGHT, BUSINESSWOMAN BY DAY

was a little girl, I'd find something to sell to make some extra change, and that continues," Jenni said. "Singing is my job. I will always be a businesswoman, but not always an artist, a musician."

In the age of the reality show, Jenni Rivera capitalized on it, introducing us to *I Love Jenni* in 2010 and its spinoff *Chiquis 'n Control*, starring her daughter Janney "Chiquis" Marin, with both airing on Telemundo's mun2 channel.

"I know I have something to say and people like to listen," Jenni Rivera told the *San Antonio Express News.* "I really feel and believe that's what my future will be, but I always thought it would be later on, when I'm done singing and ready to start a new career."

Like the Kardashian clan on American reality TV, Jenni Rivera didn't mind having people see her sometimes tabloid lifestyle.

Jenni liked the comments she would get. She said people would tell her "You're such a normal family, you're just like us," or would say "My mom is not as crazy as you."

When first approached about doing a reality TV show by the Spanish-language networks, Jenni wanted to be in control.

"She wanted creative control," Rivera's friend and manager Pete Salgado said. "I remember people thought she was out of her mind because mun2 is such a small cable network. But they were the ones who let her have a say."

Flavio Morales, senior vice president of programming and production of mun2, recalls that Jenni didn't want to do the show

"She loved the fact that she was in control of the show," Morales said. "She was often the subject of tabloid stories, but here she got to say exactly what she wanted to say."

I Love Jenni averaged 60,000 viewers, but jumped 34 percent by its second season, with more than 100,000 viewers in prime time — big numbers for a small network. Those numbers helped the Rivera clan become the royal family of mun2.

at first, but caught the TV bug when she saw the final product.

"When we got her on camera, she was magic," Morales told the *L.A. Times*. "She knew what to say, how her audience would react and then as we started production, she got what we called the TV bug."

I Love Jenni was a sort of a "wink" to the old *I Love Lucy* shows of the 1950s, according to the *L.A. Times*. Major corporations such as Target, T-Mobile and Burger King all signed on to sponsor the hit show for mun2.

"It was the brand-defining show for us," Diana Mogollon, general manager for mun2, told the *L.A. Times*. "The network is 11 years old, but we're still in diapers. *I Love Jenni* helped us find our groove."

The TV shows spawned the fashion lines. Jenni had her own makeup line and fragrance, "Jenni by Jenni Rivera," which was sold at Sears. She also partnered with NuMe to develop a line of pricy blow dryers and flat irons. Denim jeans and boutique stores were also in the mix.

If all those products weren't enough, she had her own four-hour radio show called *Contacto Director con Jenni Rivera.*

"I'm a communicator. I want to touch different subjects — relationship problems, social issues, immigration, gossip, whatever

people are going through. I want them to hear firsthand how I feel. Plus, I get to play music and clear up gossip about myself," Jenni said. "We have a segment called 'Que Haria Jenni,' – what would Jenni do in my situation? I have a forgiveness section. If

there's somebody that you hurt, we can connect you to that person and smooth everything out so that you guys can be friends, lovers, business associates or whatever. I want to do positive things for my people."

In *I Love Jenni*, Jenni Rivera did not shy away from controversial subjects, including one in 2010 where she traveled to Arizona to march in protest of the state's SB 1070 immigration law.

"My name is Jenni Rivera. I speak Spanish perfectly and I speak English perfectly. At least I try," she told those gathered for the rally, according to the *Whittier Daily News.* "I was proudly born and raised in the L.A. area, raised in Long Beach, California and at 10 in the morning, I was proudly marching with you guys. That wasn't the artist. That was a proud, Mexican female standing up for her people."

Feature films were next on Jenni's hit list. In April 2012, Jenni began her English

acting debut in the movie *Filly Brown*, an independent drama in which she played the imprisoned mother of an aspiring rapper, who is trying to stay connected to her daughter while behind bars.

Filly Brown was nominated for the Grand Jury Prize at the 2012 Sundance Film Festival and won Best Feature Film at the 2013 Noor Iranian Film Festival. Her co-stars were Edward James Olmos, Lou Diamond Phillips and Gina Rodriguez.

"Jenni was an amazing force," Olmos told *Billboard*. "From the very beginning I've said that she could garner an Academy Award for her work in *Filly Brown*. She had a tough life, but she also had an extraordinary gift."

In short, Jenni Rivera's business sense was as top notch as her singing ability.

"When I saw that my life provoked interest or intrigue among television people, I thought, 'I am going to use my name my way.' My name is used in many ways by many people, so then the best way to employ the name of Jenni Rivera is to be the businesswoman I am and say, 'I am going to produce television programs, I will have

market something.' That's something that always stayed in my head. Never did I imagine that I would sell myself. Everything is the result of the music, but the business mind came before. The two joined up, and together we created an entertainer," Jenni said.

a clothing line, I will create fragrances, I will have my own radio program,'" said Jenni during the *Billboard* Latin-music conference in April 2012.

"I think I'm a better businesswoman than an artist. Whether selling chewing gum in school or selling my grades and test answers in class, I was always selling something," Jenni told Leila Cobo in an interiew in 2012.

Jenni Rivera attributes her business sense to a teacher in business school.

"My teacher at the business school told me, 'You must sell something, you must

CHAPTER FIVE:

THE DOOMED FLIGHT OF LEARJET 25

In 1971, American folk rock singer-song-writer Don McLean released the song "American Pie," which includes the lyric "the day the music died."

It's in reference to the death of three well-known rock and roll musicians who died in February 1959 in a plane crash in Iowa. Those who died included Buddy Holly, J.P. "The Big

seen, but the day she died in a plane crash on December 9, 2012, in Northern Mexico sure feels like a "day the music died."

So, what exactly happened on that day? This is what we know.

Following a concert in Monterrey, Nuevo Leon, Mexico, Jenni Rivera boarded the plane in the early morning hours of

Bopper" Richardson and Ritchie Valens.

Valens, who is known for the hit "La Bamba," could be considered the first Mexican-American rock and roll superstar. The Los Angeles native was only 17 years old when he died. "American Pie," is a classic song that has endured over the years.

Whether or not a song will ever be written on the death of Jenni Rivera remains to be

December 9, 2012. According to *Billboard*, Rivera was traveling with Arturo Rivera, Jorge "Gigi" Armando Sanchez Vasquez, Jacobo Yebale, Mario Macias Pacheco, along with pilot Miguel Perez Soto and co-pilot Alejandro Jose Torres.

Arturo Rivera was Jenni's publicist, but they were not related. Arturo Rivera was a journalist-turned-publicist and was very well

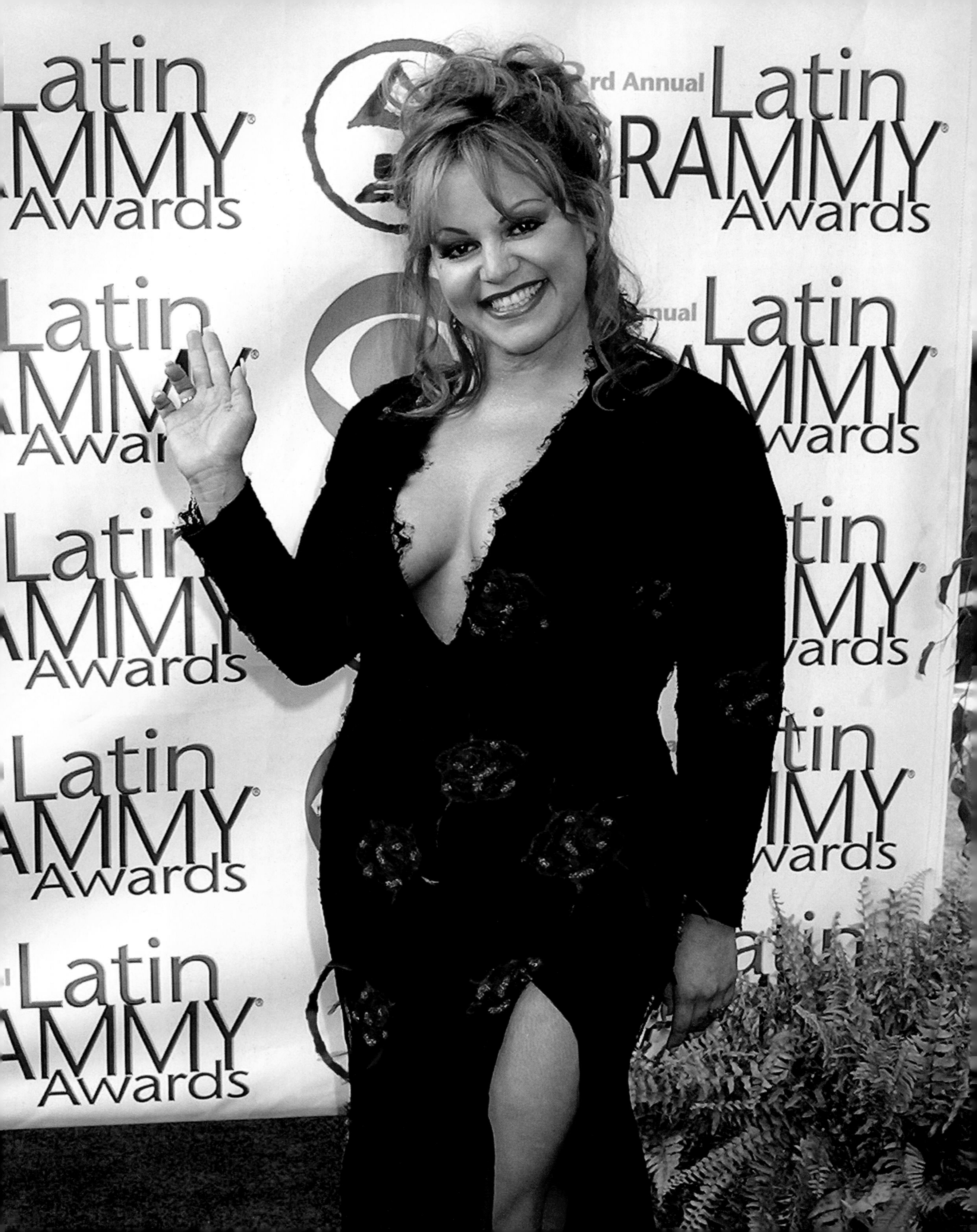
rd Annual
Latin
Awards

known in the entertainment business. He was said to be at the "zenith" of his career and had a regular, recurring segment on *El Gordo y La Flaca*, reporting about regional Mexican musical acts. Besides Jenni Rivera, he represented other regional Mexican music entertainers including Larry Hernandez and Banda El Recodo. "He (Arturo Rivera) was by far the most important publicist in grupero music," said Teresa Aguilera, a correspondent for *Billboard* in Mexico. "He was a very charismatic individual." Arturo Rivera was the founder of AR Productions, a public relations firm, together with his sister Cynthia Rivera and Mario Larios.

Jenni's make-up artist Jacobo Yebale, a native of Guadalajara, Mexico, had also worked for Christina Aguilera, Brett Michaels, Rihanna, Don Omar and Pitbull. Yebale was one of the most sought after make-up artists in the entire United States, with stars postponing photo shoots and even sending private aircrafts to pick up Jacobo in order to assure his availability. Moments before the plane crash happened, Yebale posted to Instagram what is believed to be the last known photo of Rivera alive. He wrote on the caption: "We're getting Back To Mexico City ... Jenni Rivera, Arturo, Gigi and

Me .. Los Amooo! [I love you]"

"Gigi" was Jorge Sanchez, Jenni Rivera's official hair stylist.

Marcías was Rivera's attorney in Mexico.

At the time of the crash, Rivera was traveling from a concert at the Monterrey Arena to shoot an episode of *La Voz*, the Mexican version of *The Voice*. She was one

"There is nothing recognizable, neither material nor human" in the wreckage found in the state of Nuevo Leon, Transportation and Communications Minister Gerardo Ruiz Esparza told reporters. "The impact was so powerful that the remains of the plane "are scattered over an area of 250 to 300 meters. It is almost unrecognizable."

Jenni Rivera's father, Pedro Rivera, told

of the celebrity coaches. Shortly after 3 a.m., the Learjet took off from the airport near Iturbide, but would soon lose contact with the air traffic control tower. By 3:25 a.m., the Learjet was traveling at 35,000 feet at some 600 miles per hour when it nose-dived into a mountainous terrain, killing all on board.

reporters, "I believe my daughter's body is unrecognizable." Among the few things found was a mangled California driver's license with Rivera's name and photo found near the crash site. Mexico's General Civil Aviation Administration (DGAC) lead the investigation into the crash, along with the

system in the wings, "resulting in one side of the plane experiencing a loss in balance."

In the 2005 report, the captain noted that the "alignment to runway was off due to right wing." He said that "subsequently, the airplane exited the left side of the runway striking a runway distance marker," resulting in substantial damage. No one was injured in the accident.

U.S. National Transportation Safety Board assisting the National Transportation Safety Board conducted an investigation into the crash.

The Huffington Post said the NTSB reported that the Learjet 25 was involved in one previous accident in 2005. It struck a runway marker while trying to land at an airstrip in Amarillo, Texas on July 1, 2005.

According to the FAA report, the Learjet 25 was "substantially damaged when it struck a runway distance marker following a loss of directional control while landing." The NTSB report describes a malfunction with the fuel

The aftermath of the fatal crash seemed to play out in controversy, just like much of Jenni Rivera's life seemed to have attracted when she was alive. Soon after the crash, and as the investigation continued, family members of publicist Arturo Rivera, Jacobo Yebale, attorney Mario Macias and Jorge "Gigi" Sanchez all filed a lawsuit against Starwood Management LLC., Rodatz Financial Group, Inc., the owners of the plane, and the previous owner of the plane, Mcoco, Inc., as well as Jenni Rivera Enterprises.

The lawsuit was filed in the Superior Court of Los Angeles on January 10, 2013, not even a month following the crash. "Because all of them could possibly be responsible and we know that it wasn't Arturo and Jacob, or counselor Macías; they weren't in charge of choosing that plane," Vance Owen, attorney for the plaintiffs, told the Huffington Post Voces. "Now we're looking into the possibility that someone with Jenni Rivera's company had something to do with choosing to rent that plane that was a piece of junk."

Another attorney on the case, Paul Kiesel, told the *L.A. Times*, "We cast a wide net to find out exactly who is responsible, and it may be that they're not. We have named Rivera Enterprises, who likely arranged the charter of this plane — in hindsight a very bad decision." The attorney for the families didn't put a dollar amount of how much they were seeking in the lawsuit, although the defendants may have to pay millions.

"It's too soon to say, this is not just about money but to seek answers and know what happened," Owen told Voces.

The lawsuit calls for "compensation for damages" from everyone involved with the hiring and renting of the 43-year-old, fixed-wing, multi-engine aircraft with a "long history of maintenance problems and prior 'substantial' left wing and airframe structural damage."

Ironically, the airplane was originally manufactured and certified to fly on December 9, 1969, 43 years to the day of the crash that claimed the 43-year-old Jenni Rivera's life. "The Learjet was such an old airplane that it was referred to in the aviation community as a 'bucket of bolts,'" according to the lawsuit.

"I'm not going to profit from this situation, I'm not going to hurt [Jenni Rivera's] family, and her children, this is only part of the investigation. I am not seeking to damage them because they are going through the same mourning that I am going through," said Cynthia Rivera, sister of publicist Arturo Rivera, told the Univision talk show *El Gordo y La Flaca*. Cynthia Rivera's father, Agustin Rivera Jaime, is the plaintiff in the lawsuit for his son Arturo Rivera.

The lawsuit states Mcoco put the Learjet up for sale and sold it to Starwood and Rodatz on June 1, 2012. According to the lawsuit, pilot Miguel Perez Soto and co-pilot Alejandro Jose Torres of the doomed plane were "selected, hired, trained, supervised and employed by Starwood and Rodatz."

The lawsuit states that Soto, who was 78 years old at the time of the crash, was licensed to fly under a limited and temporary airman certificate issued in October 2010. The license forbid operation of a Learjet on flights which carried any passenger for hire or on flights proceeding under instrument flight rules conditions.

Meanwhile, the co-pilot, Alejandro Jose Torres, was just 20 years old and was only licensed to fly under an airman certificate issued on April 2010, which, like Soto, forbade him to fly any passengers for hire or needing instrument flight rules conditions,

and its parent company Rodatz Financial Group. Loaiza was a professional baseball pitcher for several teams in his career, including the Chicago White Sox, Oakland A's and the Los Angeles Dodgers. Although Rivera filed for divorce from him two months before the plane crash, the AP reported that he continued to receive financial benefits from her.

Loaiza's complaint alleges the 78-year-old pilot and the co-pilot weren't licensed to fly paying passengers.

the lawsuit states. According to the *L.A. Times*, executives with Starwood told the newspaper after the crash that the jet was "perfectly maintained."

The lawsuit is expected to be tried in California, a L.A. county judge ruled, although the plane operators tried moving the case to Mexico.

This is not the only lawsuit filed following the plane crash. In February 2014, the Associated Press reported that the former husband of Jenni Rivera, Esteban Loaiza, filed a wrongful death lawsuit against the plane's owner Starwood Management LLC

In 2013, Mexico's civil aviation agency issued a report stating the Mexican government violated laws by granting licenses to the pilot because he exceeded the age limit for the kind of license he obtained. The report, according to the AP, also stated the Learjet was 43 years old and had flaws such as "flying unevenly and trembling when it reached cruising speed."

CHAPTER SIX:

JENNI RIVERA
LIVES FOREVER

CHAPTER SIX: JENNI RIVERA LIVES FOREVER

The last time the public got to witness the unrivaled talent of Jenni Rivera, "La Diva de la Banda," was on stage in Monterrey, Mexico on December 8, 2012.

Perhaps fittingly, that's the way the public should remember the 43-year-old Rivera: in all her glory, belting out her now famous Banda, Ranchera and Norteño hits and classics that led to the sale of 20 million albums during her still young career.

In fact, at that concert, Rivera was presented with gold and platinum albums for her latest album, *Joyas Prestadas*, according to Fusion.net.

Just a few short hours after giving what would be her last performance of not only her career, but of her life, the Learjet 25 that carried Jenni Rivera and six others plunged 28,000 feet over Iturbide, Nuevo Leon, Mexico, killing all on board just 10 minutes after take off.

Rivera was traveling to Mexico City and the crash ended her life in a manner that no one could have predicted, prevented or expected. How could this media mogul from a singing family dynasty suddenly be no longer with us? That's a question that

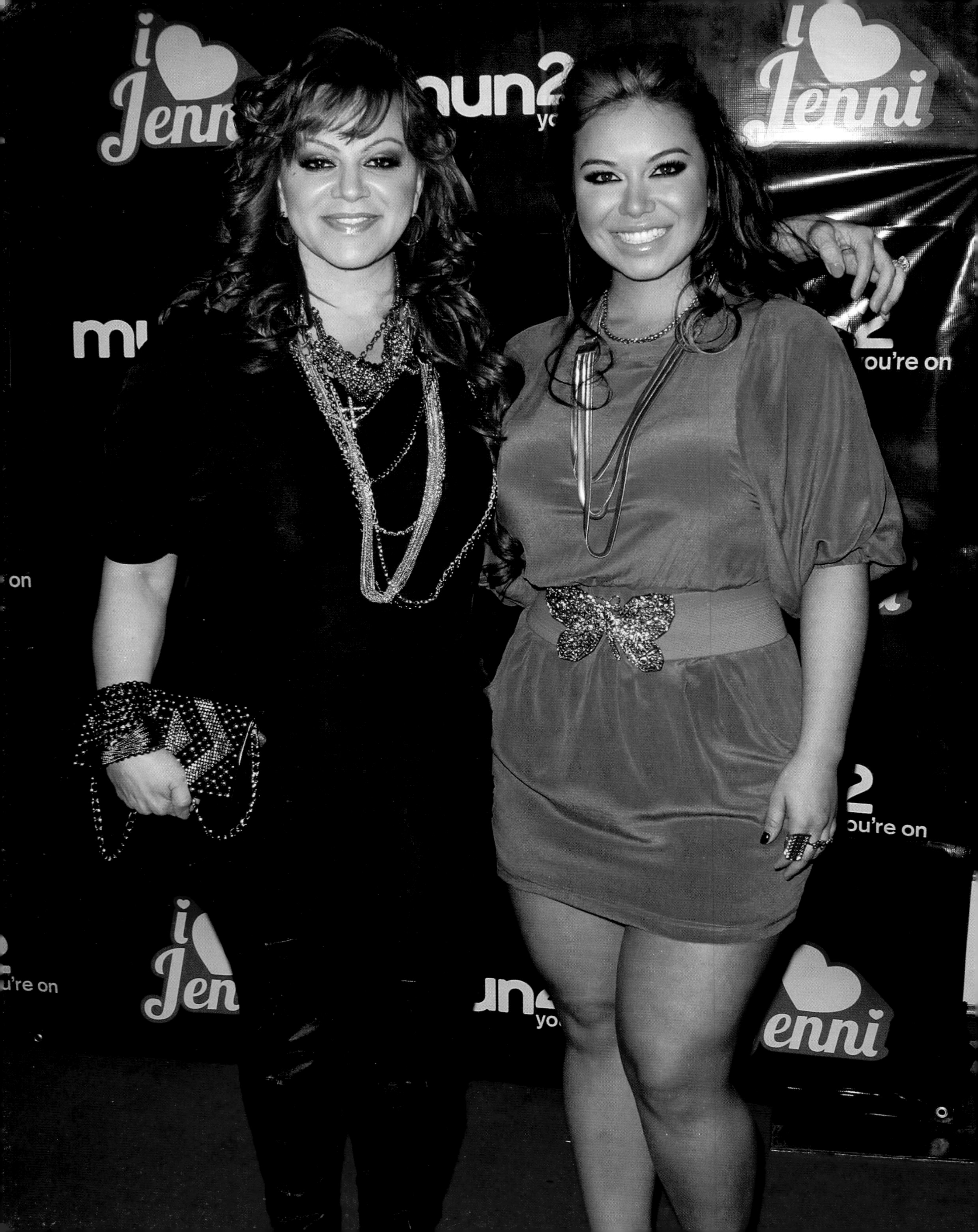
Jenni
you're on

her fans and admirers worldwide have been asking. They're also asking, what could have been?

Had she lived today, what would Jenni be doing?

"For Jenni, it was all about the promise that was yet to come," said Flavio Morales, senior vice president of programming and production at mun2, a division of NBCUniversal, which aired the popular *I Love Jenni*. Most likely she would have been making more inroads into the English-language American market in not only music, but also television and film. Her performance in the independent film *Filly Brown* was a small glimpse into what was to come.

Although she had a small part in the film, Jenni worked for months on her scenes as the incarcerated mother of an aspiring rapper. "A lot of women can relate to the fact that she's not this ingénue. She's just this woman who went through a lot and was forged by all the terrible things she went through," Youssef Delara, the director of *Filly Brown*, told the *L.A. Times*. *Filly Brown* premiered at the 2012 Sundance Film Festival.

Rivera's performance earned the respect of veteran actor and co-star Edward James Olmos.

"Jenni was an amazing force. From the very beginning, I've said that she could garner an Academy Award for her work on *Filly Brown*," Olmos told *Billboard*. "She had a tough life but she also had an extraordinary gift. She touched millions of people and she'll be missed."

In April 2013, Rivera was in the process

of developing a new comedy for the ABC Television Network. Rivera was slated to play a struggling single mom. Working on the pilot with Jenni was Robert L. Boyett, who made *Full House,* and Robert Horn of *Designing Women* fame, and production was slated to start in February 2013.

The *L.A. Times* reported in December 2012 that Jenni also had her sights set on creating a lingerie and apparel line for full-figured women.

She also knew there was an opportunity to cross over into the English language music market. "What made her so appealing is that she was born in Long Beach, spoke perfect English but focused on Latin music," said Gustavo Lopez, executive vice president

with Universal Music Latin Entertainment. Universal Music Latin was Jenni's music label and she was their top selling artist of regional Mexican music.

"It was always her dream to do an English album, but she always thought there would come a time," Lopez told the *L.A. Times.* "She always wanted to do an oldies album. She was a huge fan of Mary Wells, and she would say that she wanted to go back and do those songs and show people that she did more than Banda or Mariachi music. She said when the time came, she would do it."

Although special new projects were in the works, Jenni's contributions were not only in terms of music and business. Both near her

home and far, her work on social issues will not be forgotten as well.

"She's been a very memorable person in Long Beach," fan Stacy Monzon told *Random Lengths News*. "She started from nothing and worked her way up. She suffered a lot in her life. Just seeing her overcome a lot of things that happened to her and kind of made it work in a positive way, that's been very inspiring."

As her fans wonder what would have been in the future for Jenni, she continues to be honored for her work. In October 2013, Jenni was posthumously awarded seven times at the 2013 *Billboard* Mexican Music Awards. On that night at the Dolby Theater, Jenni won more awards than any other artist, including Female Artist of the Year for her album *La Misma Gran Señora*, which was released one week after her death.

By December 2013, as the first anniversary of Jenni Rivera's death approached, it was clear her fans, the public, the press and the music industry weren't ready to say goodbye. In fact, it's her fans and her famous friends who keep her memory alive. Many spoke to *People* for a special one-year anniversary issue.

"The first time she was on my show [*Univision's El Show de Cristina*], she came up to my green room after the show to share a shot of tequila with me and after we had a few, she grabbed my ring hand and looking at my ring she asked: 'Ten carats?' I said yes. Then she said, 'Someday I'm going to have one,' and a few years later it was me holding her ring hand and admiring her rock," said Spanish talk show host Cristina Saralegui, often referred to as the "Latina Oprah."

Other stars offered comments to *People* in December 2013:

"The funny thing is, I remember everything about Jenni. I've spent the past year doing everything in my power to not forget a thing. She was a powerhouse. From her soft-spoken voice when you first met her to her informal, tender, love and care when she takes you in. Jenni was everything her fans believed she was – she was everything they wanted her to be: open, honest, loving, real, humble, talented, a down a-- chick and, most importantly, a voice for those who didn't have a voice. I pray I can one day be a fragment of what she was and what she still remains. Her heart never left and it's with the utmost honor that I get to share these words

of a heart I truly admired and adored," – Gina Rodriguez, *Filly Brown* co-star.

"I ran into Jenni at the Alma Awards and it was the first time I had seen her since I started working in the industry. She came up to me and told me that she needed to take a picture with me because her kids didn't believe that she knew me. Haha! Her kids were fans and Johnny (the youngest in particular) ... she said he had a little crush on me. I was like, 'I didn't know you saw my stuff,' and she goes, 'Mija, I'm so proud of you. You're doing great and you're only going to go up from here.' She was an incredible support to me and a friend to my family. She and my mom had a special relationship." – Francia Raisa, actress.

"I think about Jenni often and relive many of the moments we spent together in my head – especially with the anniversary of her death this week. She was a part of my life when my son was born and was excited to share in the joy of motherhood with me because, as she always said, her greatest gifts were her children – nothing else was more important. The specific moment that keeps coming back to me is after her daughter Jacqui's wedding in September of 2012. Jenni pulled me aside as she was walking out and gave me a hug and said, 'Thanks for everything. I'm so glad we were able to share this special moment with my family. It meant a lot that you were here. Love you, girl.' To that I said, 'I love you too, girl.' And never

were truer words spoken." – Shari Scorca, director and executive producer, *I Love Jenni*.

"Jenni was a fierce, determined fighter that never lost her sense of humor no matter what the world threw at her. One of my favorite memories of Jenni was hanging out with her for more than an hour in the middle of the night at a deserted gas station mini-market near Kona. For the first time in a long time she could be anonymous – she said it reminded her of being a teenager. She just wanted to hang out, drink 40s, buy snacks and crack jokes. That was our Jenni." – Edward J. Paige, Executive Producer, *I Love Jenni*.

***

In December of 2013, Fonovisa released the first of three highly anticipated albums: *1969 – Siempre, En Vivo Desde Monterrey, Parte 1*, a collection of songs from Jenni Rivera's last concert at Arena Monterrey in Monterrey, Mexico.

The album includes the song "Dos Botellas De Mescal" ("Two Bottles of Mescal"). The song begins with Rivera singing the lyric: "When I die, how I'd appreciate it if you put two bottles of mescal on my tomb."

"For our family, it's a pleasure sharing this treasure with fans of our mother, daughter and sister," Rosie Rivera, Jenni's sister, told *Billboard*. "This effort has brought us tears and made us proud and now it gives us much happiness to continue with the company that worked with Jenni in other large projects. In honor and tradition to what Jenni Rivera is, we remain loyal to those whom have been loyal to her."

On December 9, 2013, Jenni's family also hosted a live concert in Mexico that paid tribute to the late singer and featured a number of celebrities, including Tito el Bambino and Marisela.

"Jenni Rivera will always be present in our lives through her music," said Victor Gonzalez, president of Universal Music Latin Entertainment, the parent company of Fonovisa. "It is now our work to share with audiences many songs that Jenni left. Thanks to this new agreement, we have made a

CHAPTER SIX: JENNI RIVERA LIVES FOREVER

commitment to Rosie Rivera (Jenni Rivera's sister) and the rest of Jenni's family that her music will remain alive."

In the summer of 2014, UMLE released *1969 – Siempre, En Vivo Desde Monterrey, Parte 2.*
Part 3 will be released in December 2014.

Perhaps the most heavily anticipated project yet to be released will be the Jenni Rivera movie.

In late 2013, *E! News* reported that Jenni's oldest daughter, Janney "Chiquis" Marin, will play the role of her mother. The film will be centered on the peak of her mother's career, according to Univision. To prepare, the 28-year-old Janney has been taking acting and dancing lessons. However, in the weeks leading up to the movie announcement, Chiquis had to deny rumors that she was having an affair with her stepfather and Jenni's third husband, Esteban Loaiza. "It was a misunderstanding," she said.

Pete Salgado, Rivera's manager and an executive producer on *I Love Jenni*, says there's no way Jenni's memory will ever be forgotten. "Her legacy and story will be told. There will be a lot of people who have heard the name because of the tragic accident, but once they dig in to find the woman, we hope she'll continue inspiring through her story," Salgado told the *Hollywood Reporter*.

In the end, it seems Jenni Rivera's work as a humanitarian, singer, songwriter and businesswoman, will always be missed and never forgotten.

"I am a woman like any other and ugly things happen to me like any other women," Rivera told reporters at her final press conference following her December 8 concert in Monterrey. "The number of times I have fallen down is the number of times I have gotten up."